Brazilian Foods & Culture

by Jennifer Ferro

The Rourke Press, Inc.

Vero Beach, FL 32964

On the Cover: *Brazilians welcome Carnival with floats carrying dancers and musicians.*

Photo Credits: Cover photo, p. 35 CORBIS/Stephanie Maze; p. 4 EyeWire; p. 6 CORBIS/ Wolfgang Kaehler; p. 8 Omni-Photo/Jeff Greenberg; p. 10 Len Kaufman; p. 12, 24, 34 PhotoDisc; p. 13 Reuters/Vanderlei Almeida/Archive Photos; p. 16 Omni-Photo/Amos Zezmer; p. 18, 31, 38 Paul O'Connor; p. 25 CORBIS/Laurence Fordyce; Eye Ubiquitous.

Produced by Salem Press, Inc.

Library of Congress Cataloging-in-Publication Data

Ferro, Jennifer. 1968-
    Brazilian foods and culture / Jennifer Ferro.
    p.   cm. — (Festive foods & celebrations)
    Includes index.
    Summary: Discusses some of the foods enjoyed in Brazil and describes special foods that are part of such specific celebrations as Carnival, Iemanjá, and Saint John's Day. Includes recipes.
    ISBN 1-57103-301-7
    1. Cookery, Brazilian Juvenile literature. 2. Food habits—Brazil Juvenile literature. 3. Festivals—Brazil Juvenile literature. [1. Food habits—Brazil. 2. Cookery, Brazilian. 3. Festivals—Brazil. 4. Holidays—Brazil. 5. Brazil—Social life and customs.] I. Title. II. Series: Ferro, Jennifer. 1968-   Festive foods & celebrations.
TX716.B6F47   1999
641.5981'—dc21   99-24330
                                                          CIP

First Printing

PRINTED IN THE UNITED STATES OF AMERICA

Contents

Introduction to Brazil

Brazil (bruh-ZILL) is the largest country in *South America*. It makes up almost half of that *continent* (KON-tih-nunt). People who live in Brazil are called Brazilians (bruh-ZILL-yunz). The *population* of Brazil is the eighth largest in the world.

Brazil is home to the Amazon. This *tropical rainforest* covers a large area of the country. The Amazon River is the second longest river in the world. The Amazon is one of the last

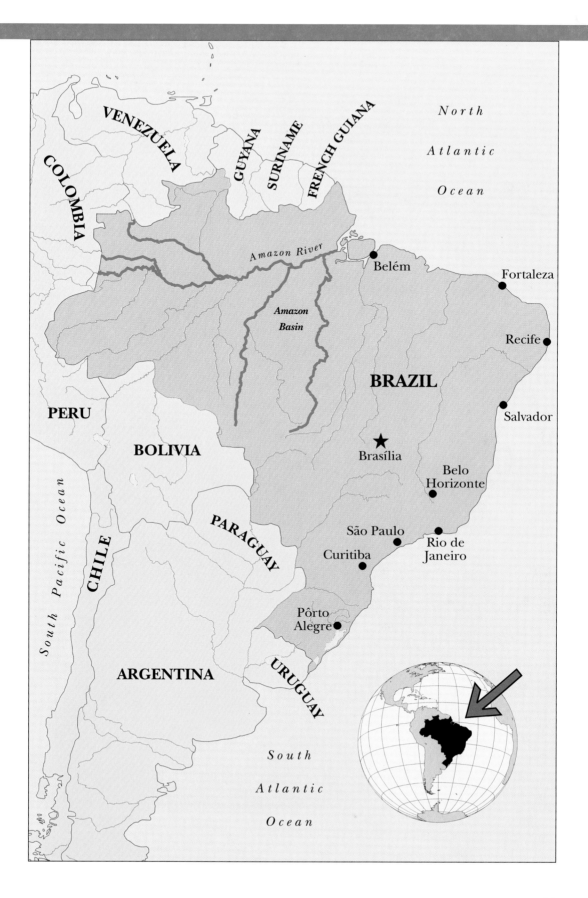

VENEZUELA

GUYANA

SURINAME

FRENCH GUIANA

COLOMBIA

North

Atlantic

Ocean

Amazon River

Belém

Fortaleza

Amazon Basin

Recife

BRAZIL

PERU

Salvador

BOLIVIA

★ Brasília

Belo Horizonte

South Pacific Ocean

PARAGUAY

São Paulo

Rio de Janeiro

Curitiba

CHILE

Pôrto Alegre

URUGUAY

ARGENTINA

South

Atlantic

Ocean

This man and young girl are from the Jivaro tribe that lives in the Amazon rainforest.

mysterious places on Earth. Many scientists believe that plants there can cure different diseases.

The *native* people of Brazil have lived there for hundreds of years. A few *tribes* still live in small villages in the rainforest. They hunt animals and fish. They speak their own languages.

Brazil is different from other countries in South America because the people speak Portuguese (POR-chuh-geez). People in the rest of the countries speak Spanish.

Portugal (POR-chih-gull) is a country on the continent of Europe (YUR-up). Portuguese people explored the world in ships. They landed on the shores of Brazil in the 16th century. Portugal made Brazil into a *colony* (KALL-uh-nee).

The Portuguese brought many *slaves* from the western part of *Africa* (AH-frih-kuh). The slaves were stolen from their homes. They were sent in ships across the ocean to Brazil and many other countries. The slaves were forced to farm *sugarcane*.

They had no rights. They were treated like property instead of people.

The slaves in Brazil became free in 1888. They could get paid for their work. They could

These teenage boys are having fun on Copacabana Beach in Rio de Janeiro.

leave the land if they wanted to. African foods and religions are still alive today. The *Catholic* (KATH-lick) religion of the Portuguese people combined with the African religions of the slaves. Today, many Brazilians believe in both African *gods* and Catholic *saints*.

Portuguese and Africans together with Japanese, Italian, and other European people make Brazil a country with many *cultures* (KULL-churz).

In 1960, the president of Brazil had a new capital built for the country. It is called Brasília (bruh-ZILL-yuh). It was designed to look like a city of the future. Together, the buildings resemble an airplane. The main government building is like the *cockpit.*

Rio de Janeiro (REE-oh day zhuh-NAIR-oh) is the most famous city in Brazil. It is known for its beaches and its friendly people. People wear very few clothes on the beach. On a mountain above the city is a famous statue called *Christ the Redeemer.* It is 120 feet tall!

A tall statue of Christ looks over the city of Rio de Janeiro.

Brazil has many *resources.* Brazilians grow many kinds of fruits and vegetables. They also grow coffee and sugarcane. The country makes its own cars. Many of these cars do not run on gasoline. They use a fuel made with the alcohol that comes from sugar.

Soccer is the national sport of Brazil. Many children learn to play as soon as they can walk. Soccer stars are very famous people in Brazil. The Brazilian team is among the best in the world.

Carnival

Carnival always takes place a week before the Catholic season called Lent. Lent lasts for 40 days. It is a time when people give up things they like. Catholics are supposed to give up meat. The word "carnival" comes from the Latin words *carne vale*, which means "good-bye to meat."

Lent is a time when everyone has to be "good." That is why Carnival is a time for being "bad." Some people call it the biggest party in the world.

Huge floats with dancers and bright decorations form a parade in the Sambadrome for Carnival.

This festival started in the 11th century in Venice, Italy (IH-tull-ee). Today, Carnival is celebrated in many countries around the world. But no country has a bigger celebration than Brazil.

Carnival lasts only one week. But Brazilians prepare all year for it. The entire country shuts down so people can dance. Large floats drive down the middle of the streets. They are followed by a huge parade of people in colorful costumes. Men, women, and children dress up in masks, headdresses, and gowns.

Samba (SAM-buh) is the national dance of Brazil. It was brought there by African slaves. Samba is also the name for the music for this dance. Samba music has a lot of thump, thump, thumping from drums. There are many different samba schools in Brazil. Each school has its own colors and its own group of people.

Every town celebrates Carnival, but the biggest celebration is in Rio de Janeiro. Street

Samba Schools

The samba school competition started in the 1930's. Schools were started by different neighborhoods. Everyone in Rio de Janeiro supports one of the samba schools. The schools are like sports teams. Fans cheer for each of them. Samba schools have *logos* and flags. Every school has a female flag holder. She always walks with a male dancer. Flag holders can be as young as three years old. The drum is the most important instrument in samba music. A samba school can have as many as 80 drummers.

parties begin at sunset. The best party is in the Sambadrome (SAM-buh-drome). This stadium holds 85,000 people. Samba schools have a parade there. It a competition for big prizes.

Every year, each school comes up with a theme for Carnival. The theme stays a secret until just before the competition. The people create a story and dance for the samba parade. Musicians are hired to write special samba music.

A dancer in a colorful costume takes part in the celebration of Carnival.

People work for many months to sew costumes. Other people construct the float for their school.

Men, women, and children practice for months. When Carnival comes, they dress up in their costumes, feathers, and headdresses. The samba school with the best costumes, dance, and story wins a trophy. The group also wins money to help with the competition next year.

Orange Salad

5 oranges
1 teaspoon of sugar
salt and pepper

◆ Peel the oranges. Try to use navel oranges because they are seedless. Remove the rind.

Orange Salad

- Cut the oranges into thin slices.

- Spread the orange slices on a plate. Sprinkle them with sugar, salt, and pepper.

- Cover with plastic wrap. Place in the refrigerator until you are ready to eat. Serves 8 people.

Meat Stew

This national dish of Brazil was developed by slaves. It was made with leftover meat parts that slave owners did not want. This stew is served with orange salad and white rice.

3 strips of raw bacon

2 onions

3 cloves of garlic or 1 teaspoon garlic
powder

1 pound of smoked sausage

1 pound of boneless beef (any cut of
meat)

14-ounce can of stewed tomatoes

1 cup of hot water

1 tablespoon of yellow mustard

salt and pepper

4 cups or 2 14-ounce cans of black beans

- Cut the bacon strips into big pieces. Fry
  them in a large pot over medium-high
  heat for about 3 minutes. Stir often so
  the pieces do not stick. Turn the heat
  down to medium.

- Cut the onion in half. Peel off the skin and outer layer. Chop both halves into small pieces.

- Peel the cloves of garlic. Chop them into very small pieces.

- Add the onions and garlic. Stir until the onions are soft, about 3 minutes.

- Cut the sausage and beef into 1-inch pieces. Add them to the stew. Cook until the meat is brown on all sides.

- Add the stewed tomatoes (with juice), hot water, yellow mustard, and some salt and pepper.

- Turn the heat down to *simmer*. Cover the pot. Cook for about 45 minutes.

Stir often. Add more water 1/4 cup at a time if it looks too thick.

◆ Add the black beans (with liquid). Cover the pot. Cook for 10 more minutes. Serves 8.

Shredded Greens

◆ 3 pounds of fresh greens (spinach, collard greens, kale, Swiss chard, or beet greens)
2 strips of raw bacon
6 tablespoons of water
salt and pepper

◆ Wash the greens. Pull out the tough, stringy stems in the leaves. *Shred* the greens into large pieces.

- Chop the bacon strips into small pieces. Fry them in a large pan over medium-high heat for about 3 minutes. Stir often so the pieces do not stick.

- Add the chopped greens. Stir for about 3 minutes.

- Turn the heat down to medium. Add the water. Cover and cook for another 5 minutes.

- Add some salt and pepper. Serves 8.

Iemanjá

Iemanjá (YEH-man-jah) is the most important goddess in the African religion of candomblé (KAN-dom-blay). She is the goddess of the ocean. Fishermen in Brazil believe she can send them plenty of fish to catch. She can make sure their boats do not turn over in the sea.

Iemanjá is celebrated on two different days in two different areas. Her day is January 1st in Rio de Janeiro. The celebration begins at midnight. She is honored in February in the northern city

This statue of the goddess Iemanjá wears her colors of blue and white.

of Salvador (sal-vuh-DOR).

Followers of Iemanjá keep a statue of her in their houses. It wears white and blue robes because those are her colors. On her day, people carry a large of statue of Iemanjá into the street and to the ocean.

People go to the beach. They dress all in white. They light candles in the sand for her. Another tradition to honor Iemanjá is eating watermelon.

Iemanjá likes mirrors, perfume, and flowers. People place these things on the beach and throw them into the ocean. They also throw in a bubbly wine called champagne (sham-PANE). Brazilians make wishes and ask the goddess to help them.

Fireworks are set off from the windows of apartments along the beach. Some people put small boats holding candles into the ocean. Then everyone dances and plays music all night long.

Other gods and goddesses are celebrated in Brazil. People give them offerings all year. Offerings are gifts to the gods. They are given to show respect. They also given so people can ask for something.

Offerings for some gods are dried corn kernels, cooked beans, and a candle. They are placed on a paper plate. The plate is left at the crossing of two roads. Brazilians believe that a spirit will take the offerings to the gods. The spirit will deliver messages from people who are asking for things.

Yuca Root

Yuca (YOO-kah) is an important vegetable in Brazil. It is also called cassava (kuh-SAW-vuh) or manioc (MAH-nee-ock). Yuca is a root vegetable, like a potato. It is eaten in many forms. Brazilians eat yuca root boiled or mashed. They also dry it and *grind* it into a flour called tapioca (tah-pee-OH-kuh). Tapioca pudding is a popular dessert. Yucas have a poisonous acid in them. The acid goes away when the vegetable is cooked or dried. You should never eat raw yuca roots. It would be difficult to do because they are very hard. Uncooked yucas have strong, thick fibers that make chewing them almost impossible.

Codfish with Onions, Garlic, and Tomato

1 brown onion

3 cloves of garlic or 1 teaspoon of garlic powder

3 tablespoons of olive oil

1 can of stewed, chopped tomatoes

4 cod, halibut, or red snapper fish fillets

salt and pepper

- ◆ Cut the onion in half. Peel off the skin and outer layer. Chop both halves into large pieces.

- ◆ Peel the cloves of garlic. Chop them into small pieces.

- ◆ Pour the olive oil in a skillet over medium-high heat.

- Add the onions and garlic into the skillet. Cook until they are golden brown, about 6 minutes.

- Add the can of chopped tomatoes (with juice). Turn the heat down to medium.

- Add the fish fillets. Cover them with tomatoes and juice.

- Cover and cook for 12 minutes, until the fish is solid white all the way through. Check by making a tiny cut in the middle of a fillet.

- Sprinkle on some salt and pepper. Serves 4.

Black Beans

4 strips of raw bacon

1 onion

2 cloves of garlic

1 cup of water

3 14-ounce cans of black beans

salt and pepper

- Cut the bacon strips into large pieces. Fry them in a large pan over medium-high heat. Stir often so the pieces do not stick.

- Cut the onion in half. Peel off the skin and outer layer. Chop both halves into large pieces.

- Peel the cloves of garlic. Chop them into small pieces.

- Add the onion and garlic to the bacon.

Cook until they turn golden brown, about 3 minutes.

- ◆ Add the water and black beans.

- ◆ Turn the heat down to low. Cover and simmer for 20 minutes, until thick. Stir in more water 1/4 cup at a time if the beans look too thick.

Black Beans and Tapioca Pudding

- Sprinkle with some salt and pepper. Serve.

Grape Tapioca Pudding

1 quart of grape juice, red or white
1/2 cup of instant tapioca pudding mix
1/4 teaspoon of salt
whipped cream

- Fill a pan 1/4 full with water. Place another pan on top or inside. This makes a double boiler.

- Pour the grape juice into the top pan. Turn the heat to medium-high.

- Sprinkle in the tapioca pudding mix and salt when the grape juice is hot. Cook until the tapioca turns clear. Follow the directions on the package.

- Pour the mixture into pudding glasses or wine glasses. Place them in the refrigerator.

- Add whipped cream on top when the pudding is firm. Serves 6.

Watermelon

1 large watermelon

- Pick a watermelon by thumping on the shell with your thumb. It is ripe if it sounds hollow—more like a drum than a knock on the door.

- Cut the watermelon into thick slices. Cut these slices across the middle to make half circles.

- Take a bite. Enjoy!

Saint John's Day

Saint John's Day is a festival celebrated on June 24th. It remembers the death of Saint John the Baptist, a Catholic saint. Saint John's Day is a day just for children.

In southern Brazil, Saint John's Day is a big party. In northern Brazil, people are more religious. They go to church on this day. All children in Brazil celebrate Saint John's Day, even if they are not Catholic.

Schools and churches sponsor the Saint John's

Children make green-and-yellow flags and streamers for Saint John's Day.

Day festivals. Children and adults dress in costumes. The costumes are usually clothes that people used to wear in the countryside many years ago. Girls wear colorful flowered dresses. Boys wear straw hats.

Neighborhoods shut down the streets. Everyone waits for nighttime. Once it is dark, people light a huge *bonfire* in the middle of the festival grounds. In Brazil, June is the middle of winter. So it is not too hot to light a big fire. Fireworks light up the sky as people dance around the bonfire.

The whole town is invited to the party. Large tents are set up. A few days before Saint John's Day, children paint flags in green and yellow. These are the colors of the Brazilian flag. They also draw pictures of children dancing and singing around the bonfire. The tents are decorated with these drawings and with green and yellow streamers.

Children play games like musical chairs and running with an egg on a spoon. Girls sell kisses. Boys get locked up in pretend prisons. Their parents have to buy their freedom. Children have learned special songs at school to sing on this day.

Saint John's Day is also a time for girls to find out if the boys they like also like them. At midnight, they ask these questions and ask for other things they want.

Popcorn and many other dishes made with corn are popular at these festivals. People eat corn cakes, corn pies, and sweets made with corn. There is also lots of candy. People drink a hot sweet wine on Saint John's Day. Children drink it too. But they add a lot of water to it.

The Equator

If you are in Brazil in June, you had better bring your coat! The country is the middle of winter. Brazil is located south of the equator. The equator is the area around the world that is the same distance from both the North Pole and the South Pole. It separates the top half of the world from the bottom half. These two halves are called hemispheres (HEH-muh-sfeerz). Countries south of the equator are in the Southern Hemisphere. They have winter when countries in the Northern Hemisphere have summer. Also they have summer when the Northern Hemisphere has winter.

Sweet Popcorn

20 tablespoons of vegetable oil

10 cups of uncooked popcorn kernels

1 cup of corn syrup

1 cup of sugar

6 tablespoons of butter

- ◆ Heat 4 tablespoons of oil in a pot with a lid.

Sweet Popcorn

- Put in one kernel of popcorn. Wait until it starts to sizzle. Then pour in 2 cups of raw popcorn kernels. Shake the pot over the heat until all the kernels are popped.

- Pour the popcorn into a large bowl. Make the rest of the popcorn in the same way.

- Pour the corn syrup and sugar into another pot over medium-high heat. *Boil* for 10 minutes. Add the butter.

- Pour the mixture over the popped corn. Mix well.

- You can eat the popcorn like this. You can also form the popcorn mixture into a roll about 2 inches thick. Cut it into 1-inch slices. Serves 4.

Sweet Potato and Coconut Balls

3 sweet potatoes

4 tablespoons of cocoa

6 cups of sugar

4 cups of grated coconut

- ◆ Peel the sweet potatoes. Cut into 1-inch *cubes*. Put them into a pot. Add enough water to cover.

- ◆ Place the pot on high heat. Bring the water to a boil.

- ◆ Turn the heat down to medium. Cover and cook for about 20 minutes, until a fork slides through the potatoes easily.

- *Mash* the potatoes with a hand blender, potato masher, or wooden spoon. Get all the lumps out. You need 2 1/2 cups of mashed potatoes.

- Put the cocoa, 4 cups of sugar, coconut, and potatoes in a pan on medium heat. Stir until it is thick and sticks together.

- Take the pan off the heat. Let it cool.

- Pour 2 cups of sugar into a small bowl. Roll a tablespoon of the potato mixture in the sugar.

- Repeat with the rest of the mixture. Makes 36 balls.

Pineapple-Orange Drink

2 tablespoons of crushed ice

1 ounce of sparkling water or seltzer water

4 ounces of orange juice

4 ounces of pineapple juice

◆ Pour the crushed ice and water into a large drinking glass.

◆ Add the orange juice and pineapple juice. Stir and drink.

Glossary

Africa: a large continent with such countries as Morocco, Sudan, South Africa, and Egypt.

boil: to heat water or another liquid until it starts to bubble.

bonfire: a large fire built in the open air.

Catholic: a member of the branch of the Christian religion called the Roman Catholic Church.

cockpit: the place in an airplane where the pilot sits.

colony: a country that is ruled by another country.

continent: a large body of land separated from other bodies of land by an ocean or sea. There are seven continents in the world.

cube: a small square (noun); to cut into small squares (verb).

culture: a set of behaviors—including food, music, and clothing—that is typical of a group of people.

gods: beings that are thought to have special powers.

grind: to make into a powder.

logo: a design that is used to represent a group, business, or team.

mash: to smash food into a lumpy paste.

native: someone who was born in a place and still lives there; also, someone from the original group of people to live someplace.

population: all the people in a country or area.

resources: things like money or land that allow people to do something.

saints: special people remembered in the Catholic religion for their goodness.

shred: to rip or chop into thin strips.

simmer: to cook on a very low heat.

slaves: people who are forced to work and who are not free to leave.

South America: a large continent with such countries as Brazil, Peru, and Argentina.

sugarcane: a tall, thick grass that is used to make sugar.

tribe: a group made up of numerous families from the same area.

tropical rainforest: an area that gets over 100 inches of rain each year. It is filled with many kinds of green, leafy plants and trees.

Bibliography

Angell, Carole S. *Celebrations Around the World: A Multicultural Handbook.* Golden, Colo.: Fulcrum Press, 1996.

Galvin, Irene Flum. *Brazil: Many Voices, Many Faces.* Tarrytown, N.Y.: Benchmark Books, 1996.

Kindersley, Anabel, and Barnabas Kindersley. *Celebrations: Festivals, Carnivals, and Feast Days from Around the World.* New York: DK Publishing, 1997.

Lewington, Anna, and Edward Parker. *Brazil.* New York: Thomson Learning, 1995.

Morrison, Marion. *Brazil.* Austin, Tex.: Raintree Steck-Vaughn, 1997.

Richard, Christopher. *Brazil.* Tarrytown, N.Y.: Marshall Cavendish, 1998.

Richardson, Adele. *Brazil.* Mankato. Minn.: Creative Education, 1999.

Roop, Peter, and Connie Roop. *A Visit to Brazil.* Des Plaines, Ill.: Heinemann Library, 1998.

Webb, Lois Sinaiko. *Holidays of the World Cookbook for Students.* Phoenix, Ariz.: Oryx Press, 1995.

Weitzman, Elizabeth. *A Ticket to Brazil.* Minneapolis: Carolrhoda Books, 1998.

websites:

http://www.foodwine.com/destinations/brazil

http://www.maria-brazil.org

Index